Ages 3+

Letter Tracing for Toddlers

SIGHT WORDS

✓ 100 Sight Words for Tracing

✓ Frequency Words ✓ Pre-K to Grade 2

TuebaaH

This Book Belongs To.

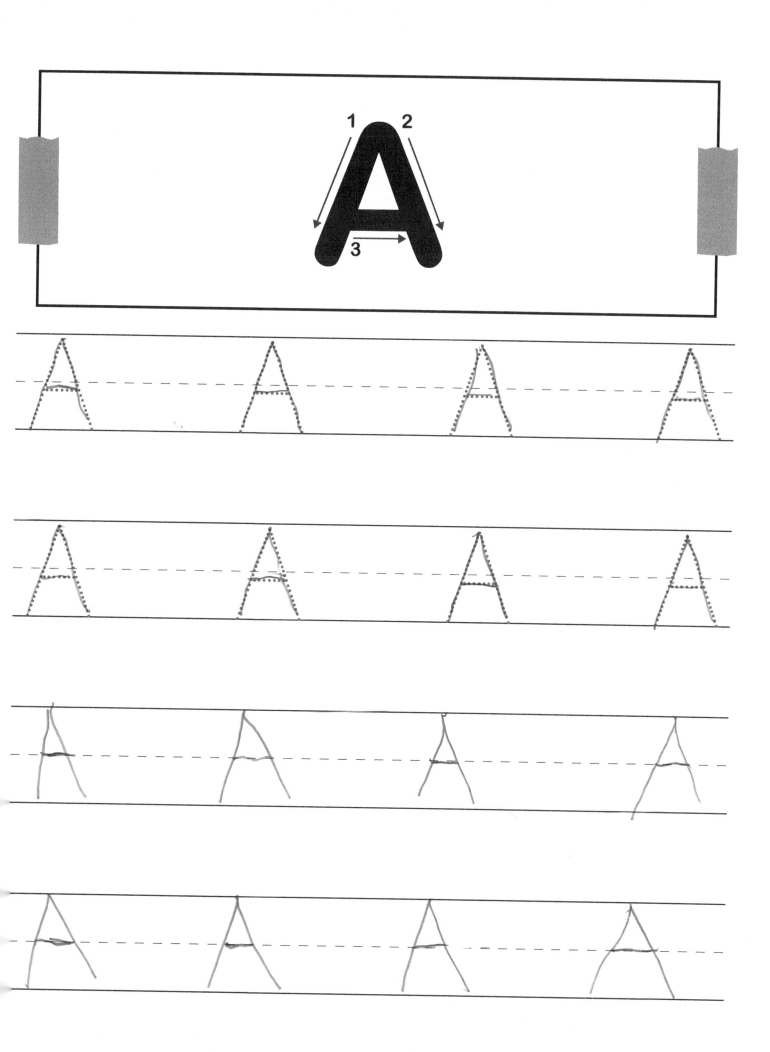

About

About About

About About

About About

About About

After

After

After After

After After

Afer After

Afer After

An

1 2

1 2

3

A n A n A n A n

A n A n A n A n

A n A n A n

A n A n A n

And

A (1, 2, 3) n (1, 2) d (1, 2)

And   And

And   And

And   And

And   And

Are

Are Are

Are Are

Are Are

Are Are

As

1 2
A 1
3 s

As As As

As As As

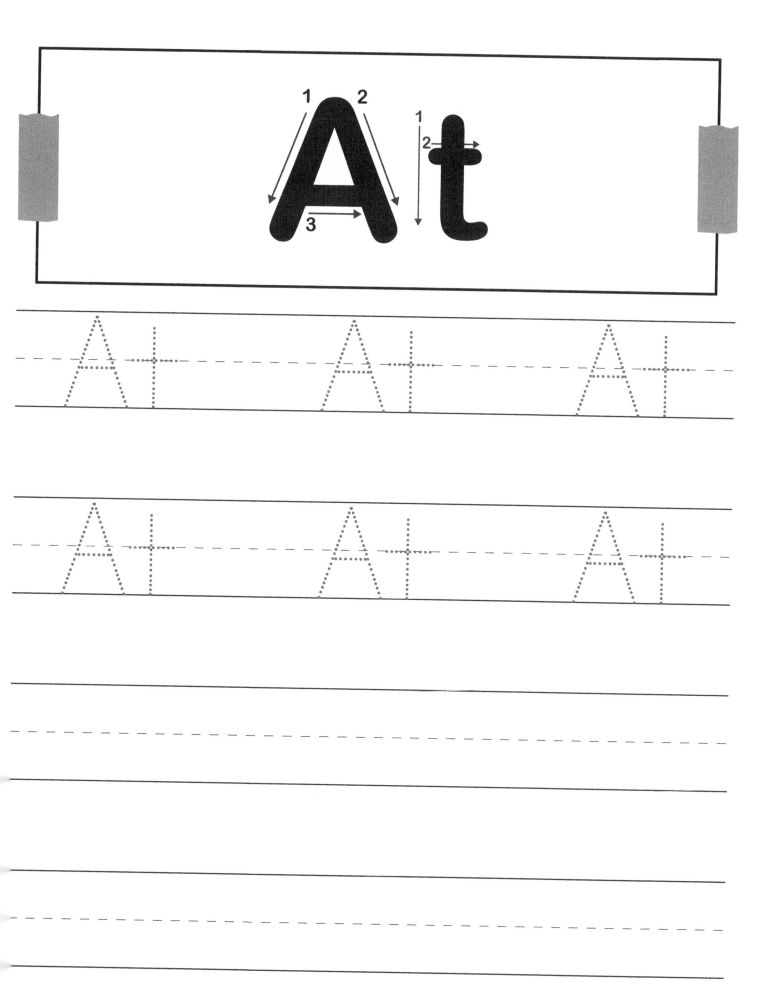

Be

Be   Be   Be

Be   Be   Be

Been

$\overset{1}{\underset{\downarrow}{|}}\overset{2}{\longrightarrow}$ B $\overset{1}{\underset{2}{e}}$ $\overset{1}{\underset{2}{e}}$ $\overset{1}{\underset{\downarrow}{|}}\overset{2}{n}$

Been   Been

Been   Been

But

But   But

But   But

By

By   By   By

By   By   By

Called

Called   Called

Called   Called

Can

Can Can

Can Can

Could

Could Could

Could Could

Did

Did   Did   Did

Did   Did   Did

Do

Do Do Do

Do Do Do

Down

Down Down

Down Down

Each

Each   Each

Each   Each

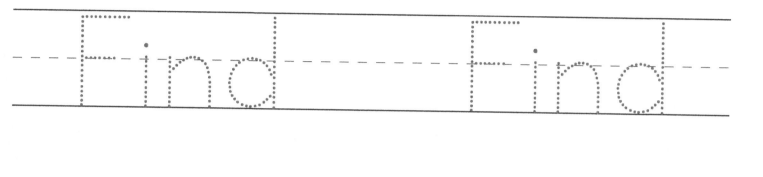

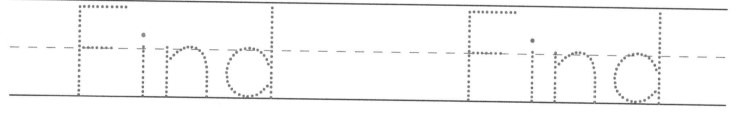

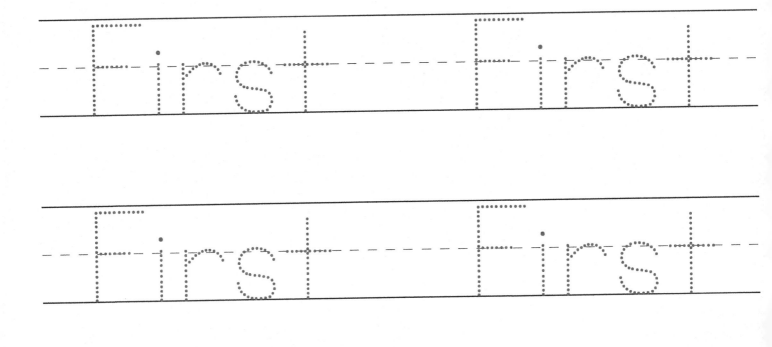

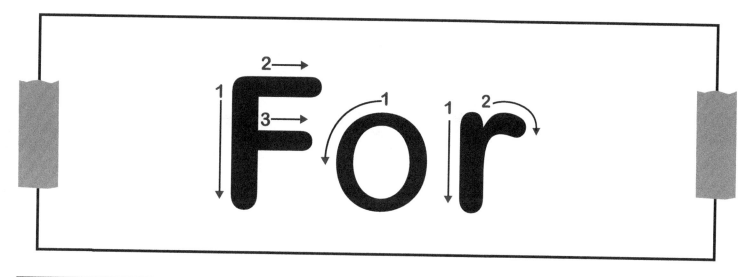

From

From   From

From   From

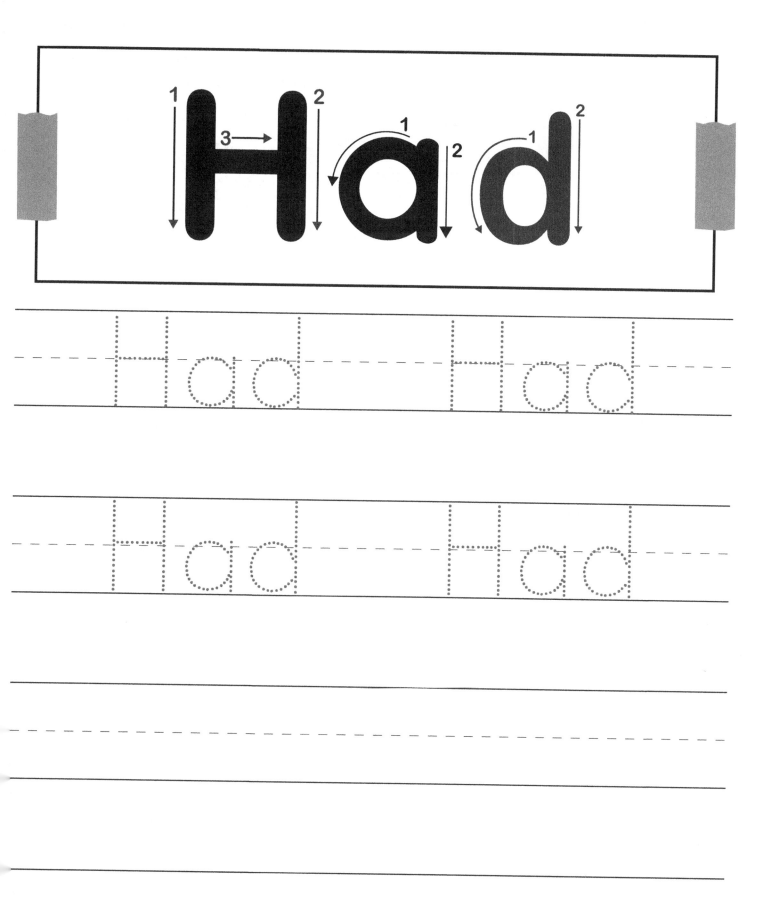

Has

Has   Has

Has   Has

Have

Have   Have

Have   Have

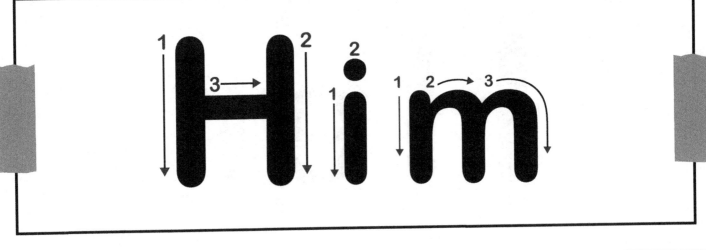

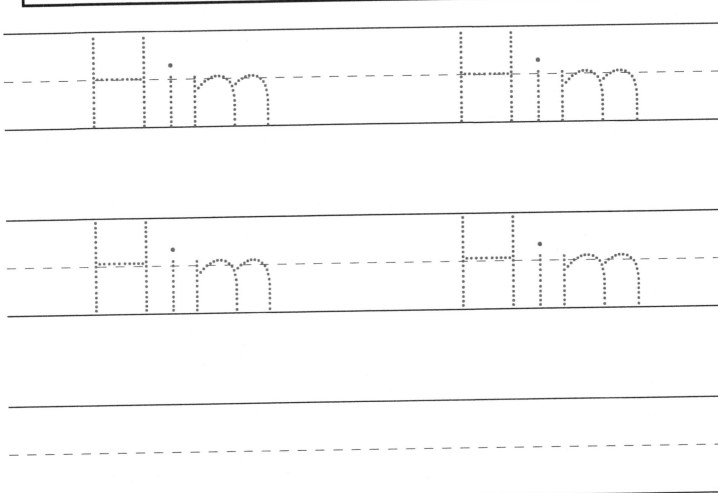

How

Hw w 1 o 2 3 1 2 3 4

How How

How How

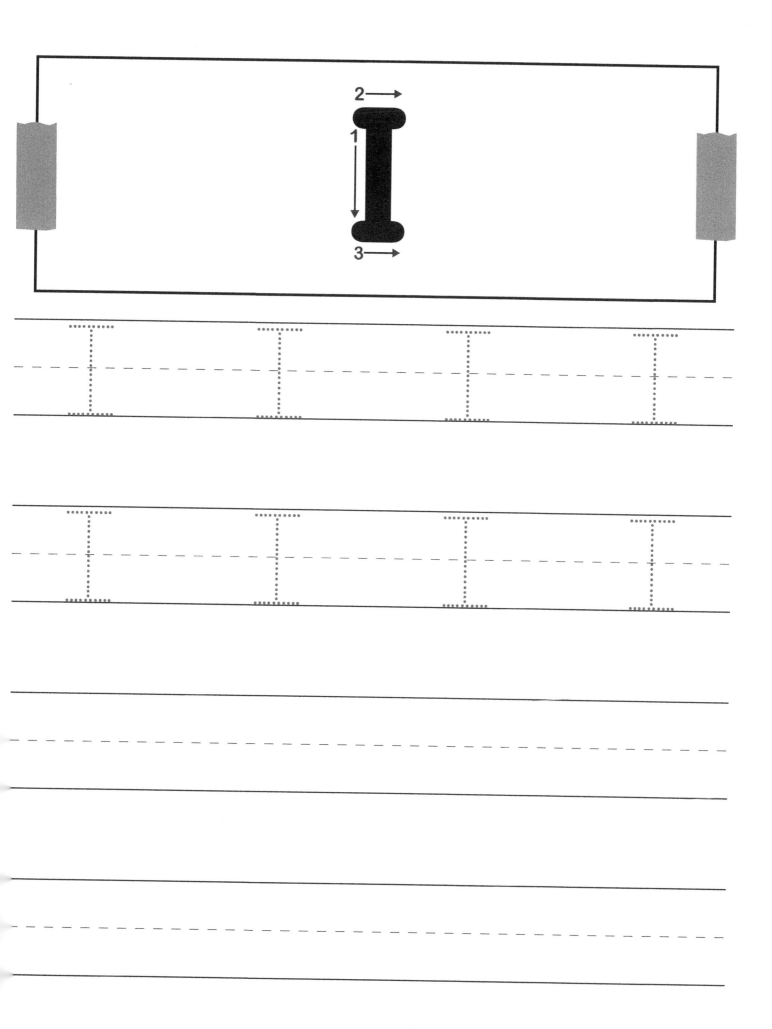

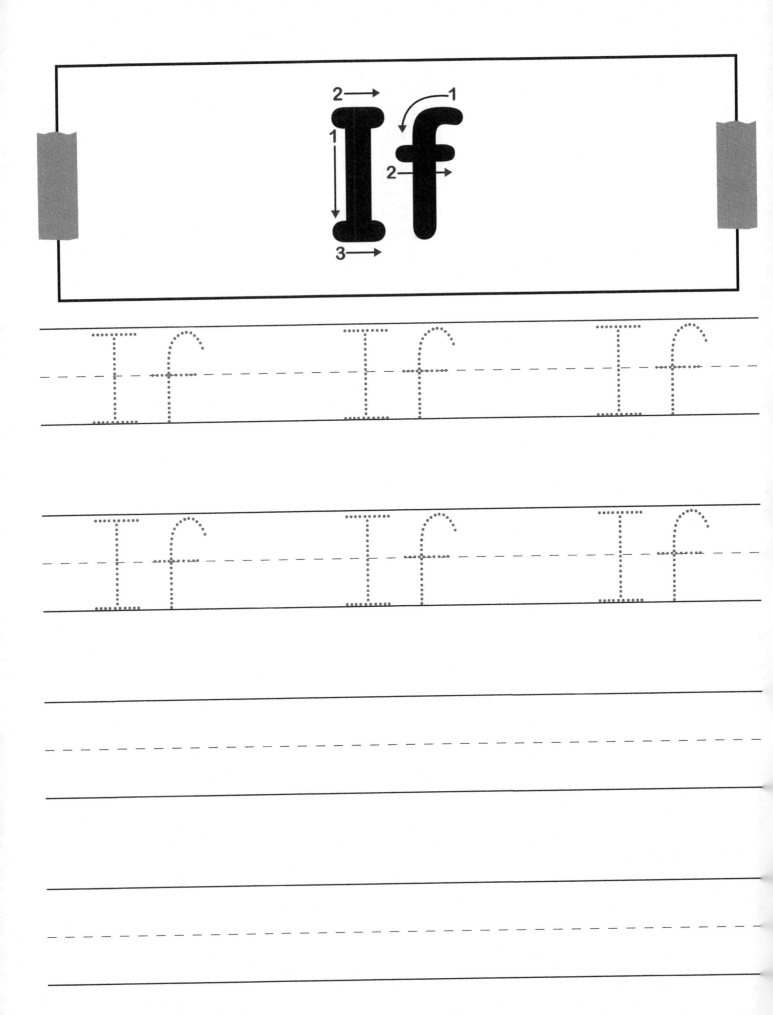

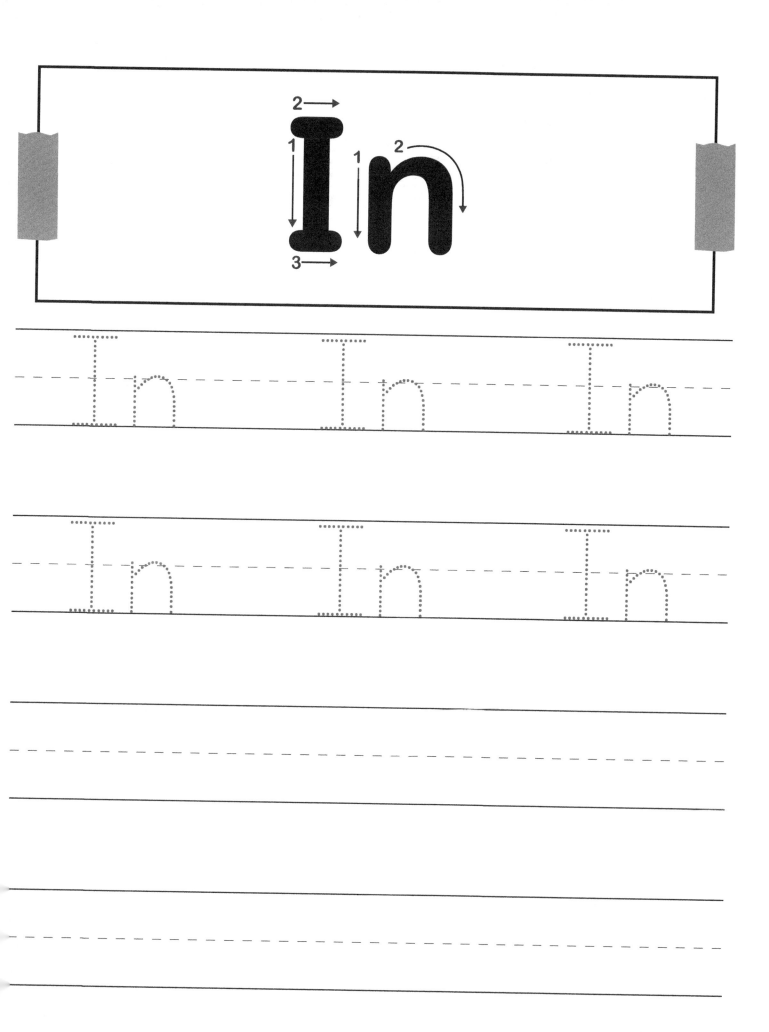

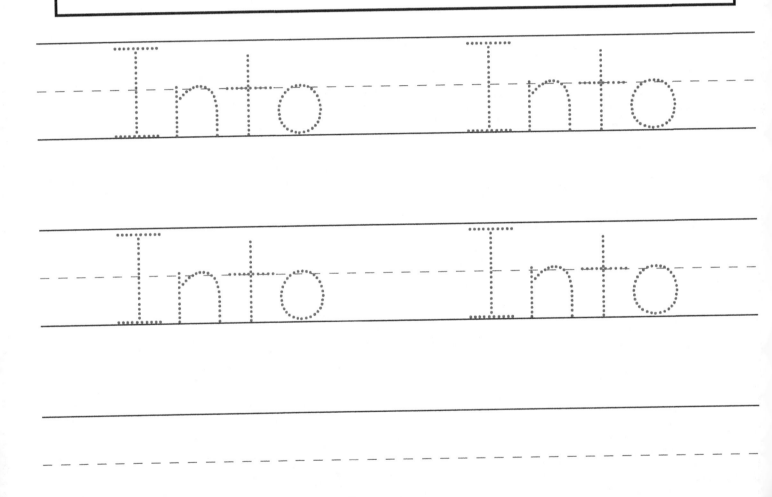

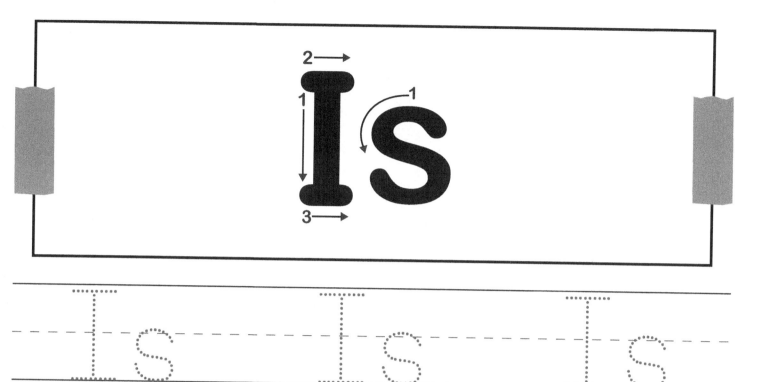

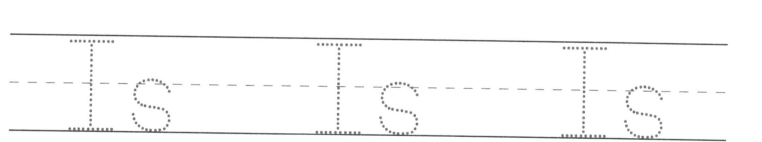

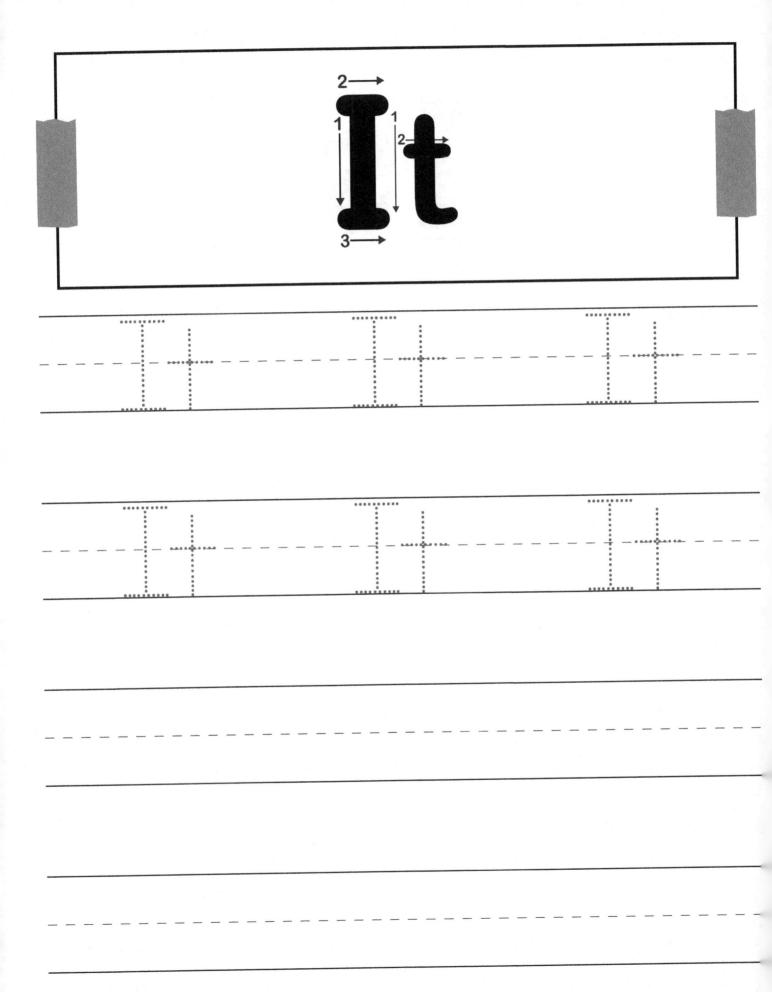

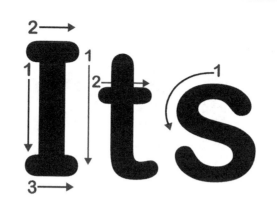

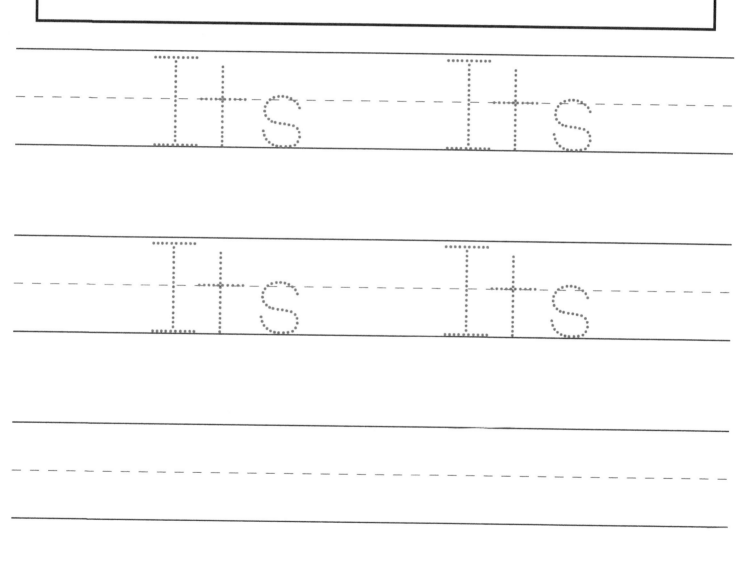

Just

Just   Just

Just   Just

Know

K — 1 (down), 2 (down-right), 3 (down-right)

n — 1 (down), 2 (curve)

o — 1 (circle)

w — 1, 2, 3, 4

Know   Know

Know   Know

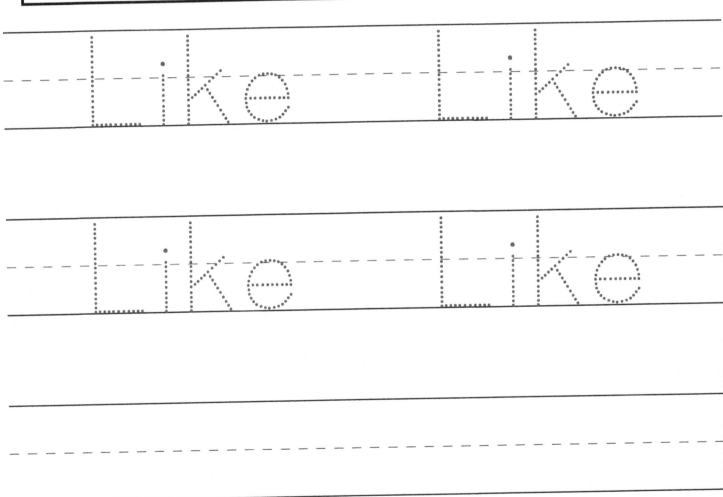

Long

Long Long

Long Long

Made

Made Made

Made Made

Make

Make Make

Make Make

Many

Many   Many

Many   Many

May

1 2 3 4   1   2 1   2

May   May

May   May

More

M o r e   M o r e

M o r e   M o r e

Most

Most Most

Most Most

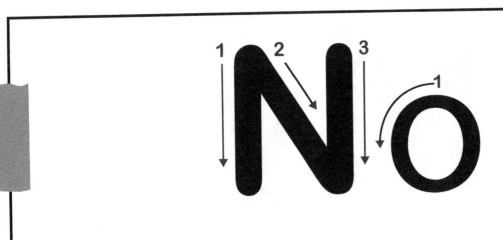

No No No

No No No

Not

N (1↓ 2↘ 3↓) **o** (1) **t** (1↓ 2→)

Not   Not

Not   Not

Now

Now   Now

Now   Now

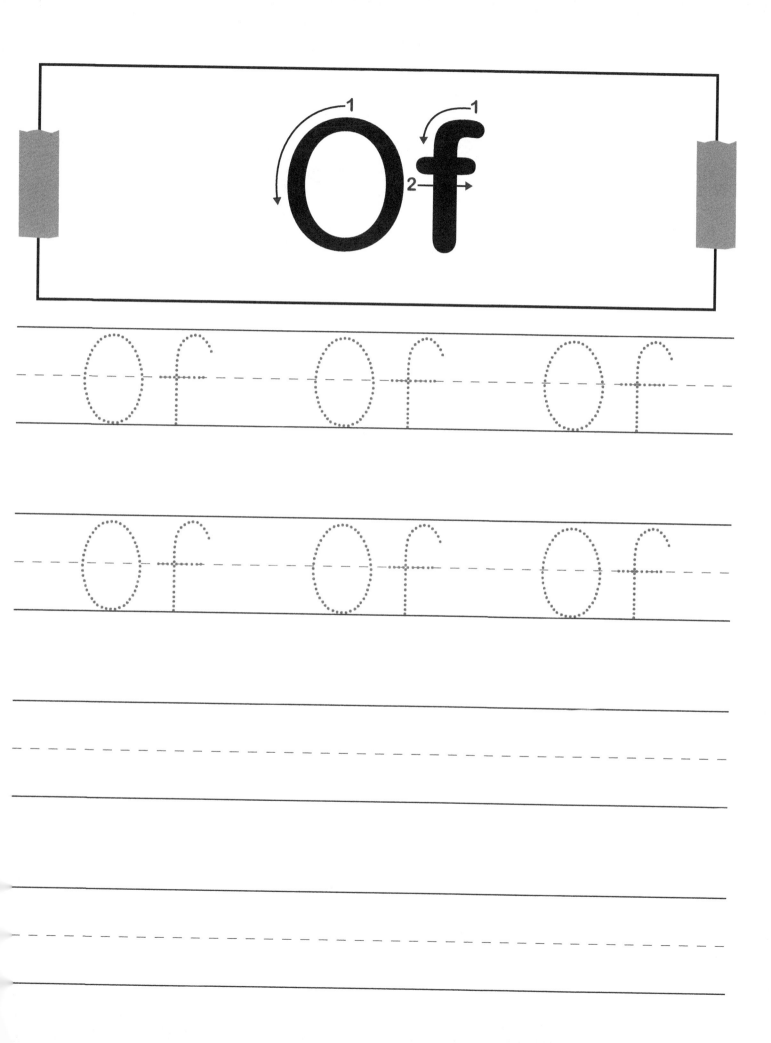

On

On On On

On On On

One

One One

One One

Only

Only Only

Only Only

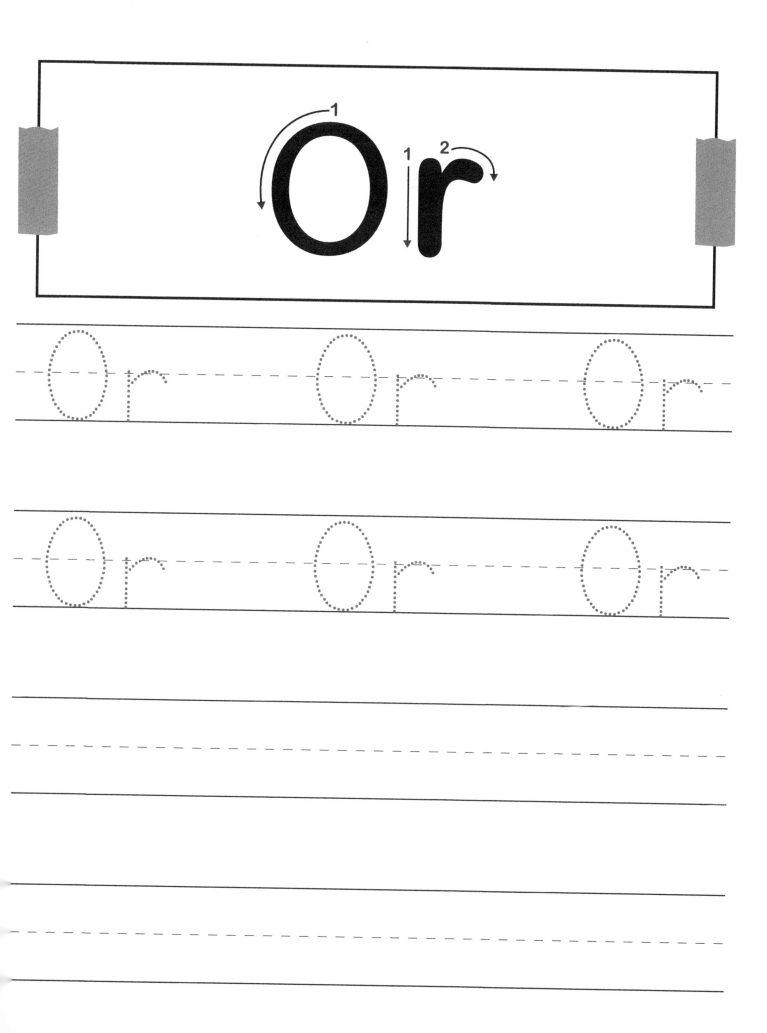

Other

Other Other

Other Other

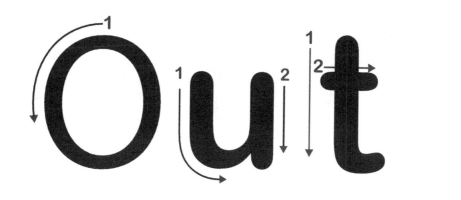

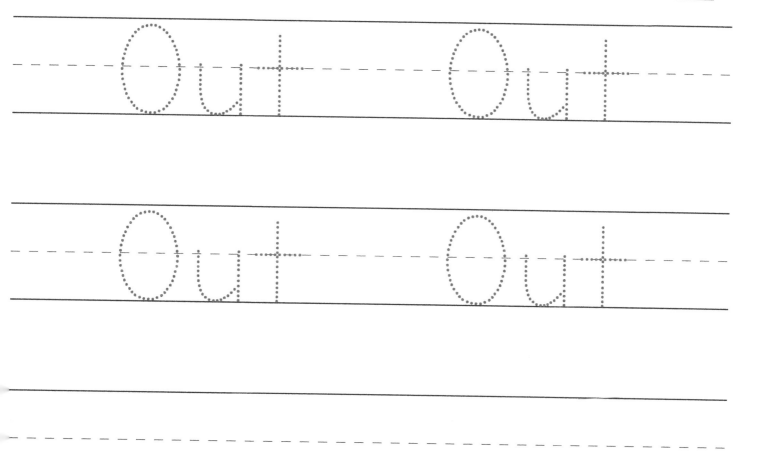

Over

Over Over

Over Over

People

People

People

Said

Said   Said

Said   Said

See

See   See

See   See

She

She   She

She   She

So

So   So   So

So   So   So

Some

Some Some

Some Some

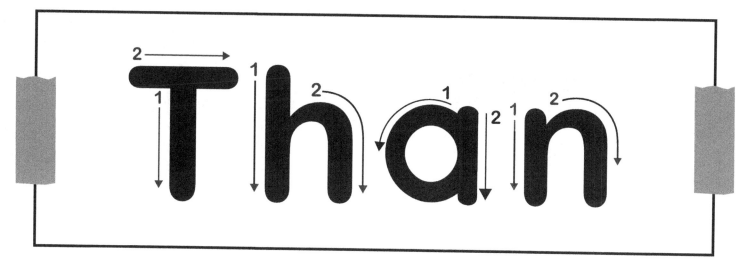

Than   Than

Than   Than

That

That That

That That

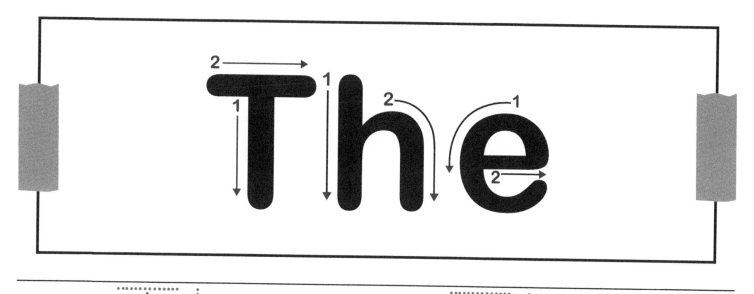

Their

Their   Their

Their   Their

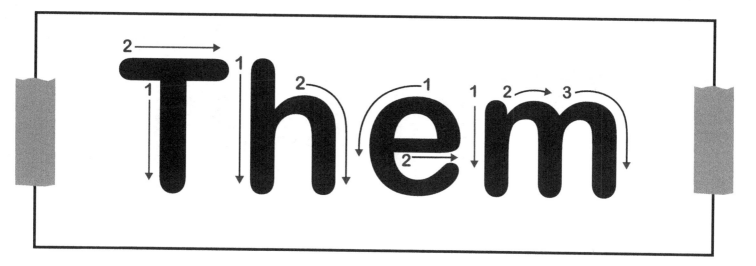

Them Them

Them Them

Then

Then Then

Then Then

There

There There

There There

These

These These

These These

They

They They
They They

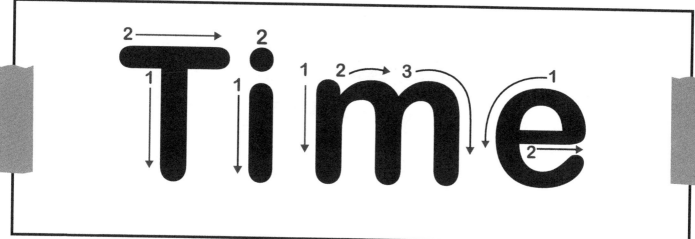

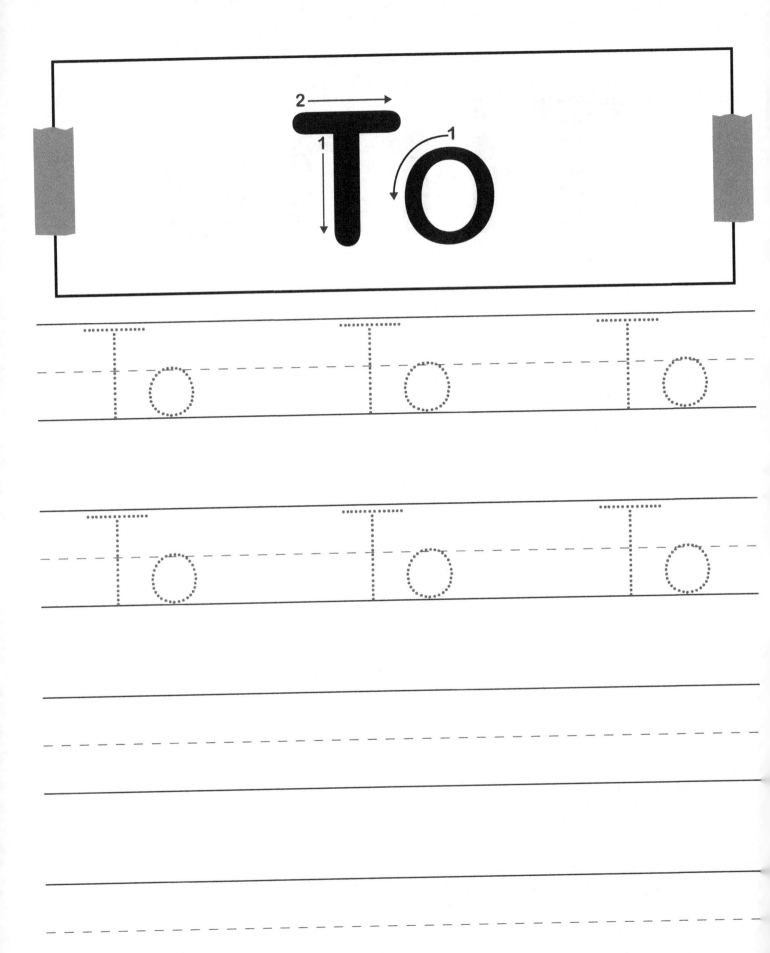

Two

2 →
1 ↓

T

1   2   3   4   1

Two

Two   Two

Two   Two

Up

1 2

Up   Up   Up

Up   Up   Up

Use

Use   **Use**

Use   **Use**

Very

Very   Very

Very   Very

Was

1 2 3 4   1   1
W a   s
2

Was   Was

Was   Was

Water

Water

Water

Way

1 2 3 4 1 2 1 2

Way   Way

Way   Way

We

We   We   We

We   We   We

Were

Were   Were

Were   Were

What

What What

What What

When

When When

When When

Where

Where

Where

Which

1 2 3 4 1 2 2 1 1 1 2

Which Which

Which Which

Who

Who   Who

Who   Who

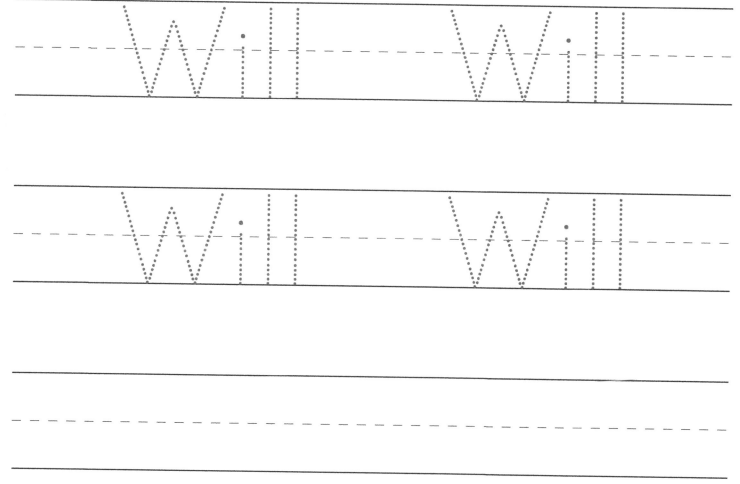

With

With   With

With   With

Words

Words

Words

Would

Would Would

Would Would

You

Y¹ ²o¹ u¹ ²

³

You   You   You

You   You   You

Your

Your   Your

Your   Your

Made in the USA
Coppell, TX
06 September 2020